Step by Careful Step

poems by

Susheila Khera

Finishing Line Press
Georgetown, Kentucky

Step by Careful Step

Copyright © 2016 by Susheila Khera
ISBN 978-1-63534-017-4 First Edition
All rights reserved under International and Pan-American Copyright Conventions.
No part of this book may be reproduced in any manner whatsoever without written permission from the publisher, except in the case of brief quotations embodied in critical articles and reviews.

ACKNOWLEDGMENTS

The author would like to thank the editors of the following journals in which some of these poems originally appeared: *Cirque-A Literary Journal for the North Pacific Rim* and *IceFloe-International Poetry of the Far North*.

My continuing gratitude for the input and support from writers and friends Jean Anderson, Marjorie Kowalski Cole, Burns Cooper, Kim Cornwall, Shanna Karella, John Kooistra, John Morgan, and Linda Schandelmeier. And special thanks to my best friend Bruce, who has read these many times and given great insight.

Publisher: Leah Maines

Editor: Christen Kincaid

Cover Art: Susheila Khera

Author Photo: Bruce Stephenson

Cover Design: Elizabeth Maines

Printed in the USA on acid-free paper.
Order online: www.finishinglinepress.com
also available on amazon.com

Author inquiries and mail orders:
Finishing Line Press
P. O. Box 1626
Georgetown, Kentucky 40324
U. S. A.

Table of Contents

Another Way to Separate an Egg 1

Summer Shower 2

Mr. Williams' Meditation 3

The Feather River Route 5

The Other Side of Fun 7

One More Look 9

Susmita Peels a Lychee 11

Homesickness 12

Acclimation 14

Are You Safe? 15

In the Shell-Shocked Kitchen 17

Gifts from the War Zone 18

The Loneliest Guys in the Pool 19

Step by Careful Step 21

Lucky are we who have good friends.

Another Way to Separate an Egg

Wash your hands.
Pick up an egg with your right
and crack it on the rim
of a yellow glass bowl.

Open the shell.
Let the insides fall
onto your palm.

How quickly
the gelatinous cushion
runs out between your fingers.

Can you feel the cool weight
of the yolk
as it warms on your skin?

You are left with a ball
the color of a ripe apricot
that trembles with your pulse
waiting to break.

Summer Shower

Years ago you swam naked
in the south fork
of the Yuba River.
Opening your eyes
underwater, you saw
foot-long trout holding station
against the silent current.

At Galena Bay, B.C.,
one blistering August day
you missed your ferry, spent
the afternoon diving
from white granite boulders
into the sea green lake.

The outdoor hot springs pool
is ringed with rocks to look
natural. You drag
your body along
the gravel bottom
like a gray whale scraping
barnacles off its skin.

Cool water streams
from the shower.
You open your mouth and drink.
Outside, dark clouds gather,
blown down from the northeast
ready to burst
and wash the earth.

Mr. Williams' Meditation

Mr. Williams, the retired
steam locomotive engineer,
waters his lawn and flower beds
while the sun sinks pink
behind soft brown hills.

He sweeps the plume of languid spray
back and forth. One by one the birds
fall silent and night rises
from the damp earth like a friend.

There was a time when neighbors sat
on the porch and watched the street, watched
evening come. The watching
kept order, kept all of them safe
and some things were safest
as secrets.

No adult children
were ever in trouble.
A missing parent
was never discussed. These days
such deliberate ignorance
has fallen away.

The teenage boy next door doesn't
like him. He runs the lawn mower
along the fence line, spraying rocks
into the rows of snapdragons.
Broken stems, shredded blooms and leaves
scatter across the dark soil.

He knows the boy's father
has moved to San Francisco
a day's train ride away.
His mother works the night shift
at the telephone office.
His older brother
plays football, stays busy.

He wishes he could talk to this boy,
he seems so childish for his age.
Or maybe, Mr. Williams thinks,
he himself is just very old.

He wants to show the boy
what type of valve to install,
globe or gate, butterfly or ball.
How to read a pressure gauge
and regulate the flow of steam.
When to bring it up,
how to safely relieve it.

The Feather River Route

Once a month throughout his teens
a boy rides the Zephyr
to the coast
of California
to see his father.

Along the Feather River
the locomotive
slows and curves
its way through the scenery.

Looking into the water
from his seat, the boy
sees trout, one
and two feet long in
the green flow below.

On the coast, he and Dad go
blue water fishing—
red rock cod,
striped bass.
Then son goes back home
traveling alone.

He visits the black cook
in the club car
who fondly remembers
venison.
"Next time you come through,"
says the boy, "I'll bring you some."

At home, all are gone,
mother, sister, brother—
working, married, football. He
eats alone
store-bought chicken pot pie
that mom left baking too long.

Two weeks pass, the cook's on shift.
From the platform the boy
reaches up
to place in good hands
the frozen deer meat
from his last hunting trip.

The Other Side of Fun

Casino signs glitter
in the noonday sun
pitching Black Jack, Keno, Prime Rib Dinners—
Joe's Southern Fried Chicken.

Cars rush down the main drag
in the desert heat
the street
a watery mirage.

Cutting its way
through rocks and willow thickets
the river finally sinks
into cracked hard earth
never reaching the sea.

1957, a third grade teacher
tells the class about her grandfather
killing Indians in his youth—
Dragged them home behind his horse.

From her kitchen window
a neighbor looks across the street
at the red and brown shacks
built in the dust, shakes her head:
They still don't know how to live.

The boys back
from Vietnam, two years
picking off peasants from choppers:
Just like huntin' jackrabbits.

In town the cemetery
is divided between
Catholics, Protestants, Indians.

Spider bites, hunting accidents, car wrecks
Our beloved, taken too soon,
kind cover stories.

On summer nights the new song
the kids all like plays
on the radio. It lasts
the whole way as they slowly drive
from the Tastee Freez out
to the rodeo grounds and back.

One More Look

Surrounding town
dirt roads are slung
over the sueded hills
like lazy ropes.

Tiny streams
dried up by August
thread their way
down the slopes.

In juniper thickets
mule deer rest
ears alert.

You and your father
glass the hillside.
Your young eyes
outdistance his binoculars.

Four decades later
up Mullinex Canyon
for a visit
you see the old campground
is trampled muddy by cows.

Away from the cover of trees
the sun beats yellow
on quartz and dry grass.

The wind moans
around boulders
changes course and snaps
like a clean sheet
on the line.

The blue sky shimmers.
This peace is eternal.

Later,
leaving town alone
you take the back highway
as the sun sets
behind barren mountains.

In the darkness
your car
is the only one
on the straight, black road.

A flash of hooves
brings your foot
to the brakes.
You see the crowning rack
his floating gait.

Backing up and stopping
you shine the headlights
beyond the barbed wire fence
that he's jumped, watch him disappear
into the Nevada desert.

Susmita Peels a Lychee

Gracefully she removes
the coarse reddish rind
as though plucking flower petals.

She hands her friend the white
opalescent fruit
that's moist and slippery
as a naked grape.

An offering, fragrant
as a rose
holding traces
of a juicy sweetness
remembered from home,
though not as fresh, not as good.

Homesickness

From your place in the corner
at the annual gathering
you sing with your tiny voice,
thin as the frays separating
from the golden herringbone and paisleys
woven through the vibrant pink
silk of your sari
that makes you look bigger
than the jeans
and pale sweaters you wear
to class and grocery shopping.

Anna makes egg rolls—
fleshy wrappers
holding meat, celery, ginger,
gives them away
at the neighbor's Super Bowl party.
You eat it like this,
she says, dipping them
in the dark brown sauce.
Like this.
Remember, I'm Filipino!

You should go to India,
the woman says,
her head moving.
Then you would know
what the things are
that we miss.

Once a year for Oktoberfest
the old-time Germans get together
and serve beer in plastic cups
sing songs they remember
from their 20's, when they left.
They watch their young grandchildren
who only speak English
stumble through dances
with wreaths of fake flowers.
If only there were good bread, real coffee,
that feeling of *Gemuetlichkeit*.

Everyone dances madly at Diwali—
Grandmas, parents, little ones
necks and foreheads sweaty
in the rented room at the community center
thick with the smell
of curry and rice.
Film music, classical, Bhangra pulse.
Dancing in circles holding hands,
men with men
women with women
rejoicing in the festival of light
when Rama returned
from his exile in the forest.

Acclimation

A young man makes his way
down the Rideau Canal
wobbling on a pair
of second-hand hockey skates
his calves and thighs
pulled by the aches
of a set of muscles
used differently.

He's wearing a rabbit skin fur hat
with earflaps.
On the street where he lives
snow is piled in berms
three feet high
after a night of city trucks plowing.

It's his first winter in North America.
The one by which he will gauge
all the other winters
of his new life.
The one that severs him
from India's days of heat
and sticky monsoon seasons,
from England's chilly fog.

He pauses in his exercise
and returns a passing skater's nod.
He watches him, the way
he easily sways his arms
and naturally shifts
his weight from left to right.
It's a well-practiced technique
that looks effortless.
He wants to make it his own.

Are You Safe?

Hopes the mother for the son
And the son for his mother.

Rows of earthenware
vases, planters, flower urns
baked dun, ochre, pink,
stacked on palettes,
the handmade exports
of recovery.

> *An orange ball*
> *shines through layers of haze.*
> *Leaving home, I'm*
> *at the beach*
> *in ten minutes*
> *watching the sun*
> *sink into the Pacific.*

In practiced strokes
I brush on the slip
that fires to a dusty coat.
Evening light glows blood red
through the muggy city air.

> *I've been here since*
> *I was five, eating meat*
> *and corn, drinking*
> *milk every day.*
> *At dusk I look*
> *across the blackening*
> *sea from where I came.*

Each finished vase
that I take from the kiln
has my handprint
on its round shoulder,
a small greeting
that I send you from afar.

> *At night, while waves beat the shore,*
> *retreat as crackling foam,*
> *I breathe the scent*
> *of kelp and salt.*
> *When I go back*
> *to look for you,*
> *I'll repeat my name*
> *(not Tom, but Tha'ng)*
> *asking, Are you my mother?*
> *Did you save me*
> *as the city fell?*
> *Until I find you.*

Shipping containers
filled with decorative
clay garden pots
cross the ocean
to America.
Maybe one day
you will come
and find me.

In the Shell-Shocked Kitchen

Years of cruel dreams-dark
chocolate, roasted chicken,
crème-filled pastries demand
that every dish be finished
clean, each pot scraped
until the metal spoon grates
against the aluminum bottom.

The butter wrapper is smoothed
with a knife to capture
the last trace of yellow treasure
and used to hold
a bite of meat from lunch.

Not wanting to eat
what is put on one's plate
is a sin, almost akin
to adultery or theft.
"You children deserve a war!"
my grandmother said more
than once, not wishing us harm,
only frustrated
by incomprehensible
appetites she thought too fickle.

Gifts from the War Zone

In Iraq
The stars were always so bright
he bought one for his girlfriend
on Valentine's Day.

From Afghanistan
he brings for that girl, now his wife
a ruby necklace and carved wooden camel
resting under a palm tree,
its lidded pack a compact jewelry box.
"It'll never change," he says
to his fellow passenger on the plane.
"We'll run out of money first."

It's late.
The night is wet with August rain.
On the ride from the airport to the base
the black streets reflect a dazzle of color.
In the back seat of the taxi cab
He's lost in the glow of his phone.

Eight months out
23 hours flying home
four months
Until he leaves again.

He walks up the sidewalk alone
to the one apartment with the porch light on.
In his shouldered pack the gifts
of appeasement, something to spark
the re-acquaintance.

He knocks and waits.
The downstairs window is lit pink.
Four months he gets to stay.
He opens the door.

The Loneliest Guys in the Pool

Laughing loudly the two
couples stroll down the rough
concrete walkway into
the pool, rumpling
the murmuring quiet
of the rustic hot springs resort.

The men are clean
as freshly laundered sheets
the women burst
with the ripeness of plums.

The brashest of them spills
himself headfirst over
the handrail, comes down with
a splash, shouts "Ooh wee!" just because
they're all out together, and it's warm.
Because they made the car payment.
Because they have a credit card.

He dances through the water
toward his pretty dark-haired wife
whose face is kind, whose mouth
is soft, tickles her till she shrieks.
"Did you miss me baby? Did you?
Did you?" he asks, breathlessly,
kissing her neck and ear. Around
his right bicep Christ's face peers, sad-eyed,
The One Way, The Only Way
scripted underneath.

At the furthest end of the pool
two young guys soak. Brush cut hair,
tattoos, one with a pierced nipple.
Adornments of the modern
warrior. They take note of
their boisterous comrades in arms.

Three girls in bikinis ripple
by, giggling, calling to each
other. The two men muster
careful smiles, look away.

The unpierced one sinks into
the water to his chin. Eyes
closed, he turns his face to the sky.
> *There were palm trees.*
> *The sun shone every day.*
> *On the road a mirage*
> *flowed like a clear stream.*

Step by Careful Step

The woods can be so dark at night
you can't see your hand
in front of your face.
Small wonder
old peasants fear that place
full of robbers and beasts.

In daylight, leaves
turn sunlight green.
Birds rustle in the underbrush.
The familiar rough trail
traverses a clearing
where wild raspberries grow.

But in the night-time blackness
well-trodden ways hold
treacheries, shift shapes.
Toes first, test the ground ahead
so not to stumble
over slippery root, jutting rock.

Raise one arm to shield
from stray whipping branches.
Link the other
with your partner, take
small steps so neither falls.
Make your way
to the moonlit field
and the road that brings you home.

Susheila Khera lives and works in Fairbanks, Alaska and has an MFA in creative writing. Her work has appeared in *Cirque-A Literary Journal for the North Pacific Rim*, *IceFloe-International Poetry of the Far North*, *The Northern Review*, *Catamaran Magazine: South Asian American Writing*, and *WoodenBoat Magazine*.

www.ingramcontent.com/pod-product-compliance
Lightning Source LLC
LaVergne TN
LVHW041522070426
835507LV00012B/1759